EMAIL MARKETING MASTERY

EMAIL MARKETING MASTERY

The Step-by-Step System for Building an Email List of Raving Fans
Who Buy From You and Share Your Message

TOM CORSON-KNOWLES

ISBN: 1631619845
ISBN 13: 9781631619847

Get free marketing tips on email marketing and growing your business online at:
www.BlogBusinessSchool.com

Published by TCK Publishing
www.TCKPublishing.com

EARNINGS DISCLAIMER

When addressing financial matters in any of our books, sites, videos, newsletters or other content, we've taken every effort to ensure we accurately represent our products and services and their ability to improve your life or grow your business. However, there is no guarantee that you will get any results or earn any money using any of our ideas, tools, strategies or recommendations, and we do not purport any "get rich schemes" in any of our content. Nothing in this book is a promise or guarantee of earnings. Your level of success in attaining similar results is dependent upon a number of factors including your skill, knowledge, ability, dedication, business savvy, network, and financial situation, to name a few. Because these factors differ according to individuals, we cannot and do not guarantee your success, income level, or ability to earn revenue. You alone are responsible for your actions and results in life and business. Any forward-looking statements outlined in this book or on our Sites are simply our opinion and thus are not guarantees or promises for actual performance. It should be clear to you that by law we make no guarantees that you will achieve any results from our ideas or models presented in this book or on our Sites, and we offer no professional legal, medical, psychological or financial advice.

TABLE OF CONTENTS

Why You Should Read This Book ix
How This Book is Organized xiii

Chapter 1. Email List Building Basics 1
Chapter 2. The Mindset of an Email Subscriber 12
Chapter 3. 11 Steps to Building an Email List 17
Chapter 4. Using Squeeze Pages to Build Your List Faster 30
Chapter 5. Building Your List and Getting Traffic 32
Chapter 6. Free, Low Cost and High-End Email
  Marketing Solutions 37
Chapter 7. Writing and Sending Emails to Your List 40
Chapter 8. Product Launches, Promotions and Swipe Copy 56
Chapter 9. Backing Up Your Email List and Other List
  Management Tips 59

Got Questions? 63
Helpful Resources, Tools, Services and Links 65
Special Facebook Group 67
Connect With Tom 69
About The Author 71
Other Books By Tom Corson-Knowles 73
One Last Thing... 75

WHY YOU SHOULD READ THIS BOOK

Email marketing has become one of the most powerful marketing tools for growing a business, yet most business owners fail to use email marketing effectively. This book will show you how.

I've been an entrepreneur since age 13 when I started a business manufacturing Seasonal Affective Disorder (SAD) Lamps out of my father's garage. I've always been fascinated with marketing. It is the art and science of attracting new customers and keeping existing customers happy and satisfied.

Since then, I've started several businesses, many of which have failed. A few have had notable success. In every case, the successful businesses had something that set them apart from the unsuccessful ones. Each successful business had a loyal audience of raving fans and customers, and a communication system for staying connected with them. Email marketing has proven itself to be one of the most reliable, powerful and scalable communication systems for staying connected with customers and fans. Connecting with customers regularly is one of the most powerful ways to grow a business. Thanks to new software systems, services and tools, any business or solo entrepreneur can implement an effective email marketing campaign right away with less than $100.

Email marketing blows away almost every other form of marketing in comparison. As entrepreneurs rush to learn the secrets of social media marketing, PR and traditional advertising, they tend to skip over the biggest modern-day marketing bonanza of all: email.

Hands down, email marketing has become the most profitable long-term marketing strategy I have seen in my career as a business owner. It has produced the highest ROI consistently over the long-term. Email marketing, if done well, can produce huge bursts of sales in just a few hours. Every business I know of that has sold more than $1 million in a single day online has used email marketing. Huge sales days are possible, especially during new product releases and launches, thanks to email marketing because you can reach so many of your customers and prospects within a few hours with the click of a button.

Why is email marketing so effective? Because once you have an email list full of happy customers and raving fans, they're basically just waiting to buy even more from you. As soon as you send an email from your business announcing a great, new product or service that can help your subscribers, many of them will buy it.

Email marketing isn't just a great way to boost sales quickly. It can also be used to increase sales every day, day after day, on a regular basis for the life of your business using an autoresponder (we'll discuss how to implement this process in your business in more detail in Chapter 7). In many cases, even if you decide to change your business, you may be able to use your existing email list to help grow future businesses. An email list is a long-term business asset, one that tends to last even longer than most business do!

While some business owners are paying exorbitant rates for marketing in traditional or online media outlets that have little or no long-term value, savvy marketers are building an email list that will continue to bring in sales and income for many years to come. In most successful online businesses today, the email list is one of the most valuable assets the company owns.

If you own a business or sell products or services, your email list could become your single most powerful and effective marketing tool. All you have to do is apply the email marketing system in this book to your business to connect more deeply with your customers, prospects and target audience.

Email Marketing Mastery is for anyone who's interested in building a targeted, high quality email list of loyal subscribers and fans. In this book, you will learn how to create a valuable business asset that will pay dividends for years to come, and help you sell more books, products and services in less time and with less expense.

If you have any questions about email marketing after you've read this book and completed the video training course, I'll be happy to answer them for you.

If you're nervous or concerned that you don't have great computer skills or you're not a tech genius, don't worry! I've got you covered. I'm going to write in simple, easy-to-understand English, and speak simply in the video trainings as well. I won't use big fancy words, and will only use technical jargon as needed so that you can understand everything you need to know to start building an email list right now. You won't need an unabridged dictionary or advanced computer skills to understand what's going on. All you have to do is follow the simple step-by-step process, and make a few choices along the way about which email marketing services you want to use based on your budget and the needs of your particular business.

If you come across any technical terms or words you don't understand, you can find all the definitions and explanations in the Email Marketing Definitions chapter.

If you don't have a budget for email marketing right now, you can still get started today at no cost. Anyone who knows how to find the right tools can start building an email list today for free. There are several free services, and I'm going to show you how to get started building your email list without spending a dime. For those of you with a serious marketing budget, I'll show you the best-of-the-best software, tools and systems to build your email list that will provide even more advanced marketing tools such as analytics, split testing, advanced Customer Resource Management (CRM), shopping cart integration, and more.

Before we get started, I want you to understand that your email list is not a business in and of itself, but it is a powerful business tool. Building an email list isn't some get-rich-quick scheme or system for creating wealth without doing any work or providing real value to society. This book is not about how to get rich using affiliate marketing or spamming people who don't want to hear from you. It's about creating a valuable and profitable connection with your prospects, customers and fans, so that you can grow your business by serving more happy customers. Email marketing is a serious business tool, and it can greatly increase sales and earnings for business owners who understand how to do it right. When you learn to use this tool wisely and achieve Email Marketing Mastery, your business will achieve profits and success far beyond average.

Ready to start? Let's go!

HOW THIS BOOK IS ORGANIZED

Because there are so many different tools for building an email list, and because this book (and video training course) is designed to be used by beginner email marketers and experts alike, there's a lot of ground to cover. You may already be familiar with some of the information in this book. That's okay.

If you want to go with the free or low budget options, just skip the sections on the more expensive email marketing options for now. You can come back to them later when your business is more profitable and you're ready to upgrade your email marketing systems.

The first chapter provides an overview of the basics of email marketing, along with detailed definitions of key terms and processes that you will need to understand in order to start building your email list.

In chapter two, we will discuss the mindset of an email subscriber and what you need to do to build rapport and connect with your audience on a deeper level in order to increase customer engagement and sales for your business.

In chapter three, we will cover the 11 key steps to building an email list. This is your checklist for setting up your email list properly and getting your first 1,000 subscribers.

In chapter four, we will discuss squeeze pages and how to use them to dramatically increase conversions and build your email list even faster.

In chapter five, you will learn how to get the traffic to build your email list, whether you have a large budget for advertising or have no budget at all.

In chapter six, we will discuss the various systems, software and options available for email marketers. We will discuss free, low-cost and premium email marketing systems and solutions.

In chapter seven, we will discuss a few ways to write and send emails to your list, and how to best position yourself and your message for your particular audience.

In chapter eight, we will discuss email marketing tips for promotions, product launches and affiliate marketing.

In chapter nine, we will discuss backing up your email lists and data, and minimizing risk so that your email list will always be making you a profit.

CHAPTER 1
EMAIL LIST BUILDING BASICS

If you have an email list stored in your email program like Gmail or Outlook, that's not a *real* email list. In other words, whenever you hear a serious online marketer or email marketer talk about building an email list, they're never talking about just some random list of people organized inside AOL, Gmail, Outlook or another email provider. In this book, we're going to learn how to use an autoresponder to build a *professional, legal, and incredibly valuable <u>opt-in only email list</u>* where *every single person on your email list has asked to be on your list and their information has been verified.*

This is important for many reasons, most notably:

You will make more money because everyone on your email list will actually *want* to be on your email list.

You will be in compliance with CAN-SPAM laws, so you can sleep well at night knowing that you are not violating any laws and won't be sued for spamming people.

You will be creating an incredibly valuable business asset that will keep you connected with your best customers and followers, providing a steady stream of sales and cash for your business every month for the rest of your life.

Your email list will be backed up and secure so that this valuable cash-producing asset will always be safe and protected.*

Having an autoresponder does not guarantee your list is secure, but it makes it a lot easier to back up your list and keep it secure. We'll cover how to do just that later in this book where you'll learn exactly how, when and why to back up your email list and protect this valuable business asset.

If right now your email list is organized inside AOL, Gmail or another email provider, this book will show you how to convert your existing list of contacts into an opt-in only email list so that you can start using state-of-the-art email marketing systems and solutions to grow your business, save you time, and keep everything legal.

EMAIL MARKETING DEFINITIONS

Opt-in

Opting-in to an email list means that a person put in their email address in a web form and agreed to sign up for the email list. There are other ways to opt-in as well, including requesting in person, on the phone, or via email to be added to an email list. Sometimes, you may hear a subscriber referred to as "an opt-in," and a web form where someone can sign up for an email list is often called an "opt-in form" or "web form."

Opt-in Form (or Web Form)

The opt-in form is an online web form that people fill out by inserting their email address, and possibly other information, in order to subscribe to an email list. Below is a screenshot of a simple opt-in form.

Autoresponder

An autoresponder is an email marketing platform and service that allows you to build opt-in forms, grow your email list, manage your contacts, send and schedule emails, and more. An autoresponder is required for anyone looking to become a serious email marketer.

An autoresponder is a service that you can acquire and access online. There are a few free ones, but most require a monthly fee. In chapter 6, we'll review the best autoresponder options available depending on various budgets and business needs.

Opt-Out

Email subscribers can opt-out or unsubscribe from your email list anytime they want. Any legitimate autoresponder will include a link, usually at the bottom of the email, that subscribers can click in order to opt-out and remove their email from your list. Your autoresponder will then tell you that this subscriber is now unsubscribed. It's not only a good business practice to allow email subscribers to opt-out, it's required by CAN-SPAM laws.

Autoresponder Series

An autoresponder series is an email or multiple emails that are sent to your email subscribers on a timer, based on when they opted-in to your list. Normally, email subscribers should receive an autoresponder email immediately after opting-in. This email will usually contain a link to your free gift (just in case they missed the link on your thank you page) and welcome them to your list. You can also create additional autoresponder emails that are sent to your subscribers on a timer; either hours, days or weeks later.

For example, if a subscriber opts-in to your email list at 2:33pm on Tuesday, they would immediately get your autoresponder email #1 (the welcome email as it's usually called.) Then, if you scheduled autoresponder email #2 to be delivered three days later, they would receive that email at 2:33pm on Friday. Many autoresponders will allow you to customize the times of the day your autoresponders are sent, so you can further customize the timing of when your subscribers receive your autoresponder emails.

Here are some examples of some creative and useful ways to use autoresponders:

Create a 10-day email course or training. Send your subscribers one email a day for 10 days that helps them learn something or inspires them. For example, if you were offering a weight loss meal plan, you could send a daily recipe every day to your subscribers along with additional tips and recommendations.

Create a series of informal, educational emails to build rapport. You can send your subscribers helpful, interesting emails to build a deeper connection and relationship with them as soon as they sign up for your email list.

Create a series of promotional emails that both educate your subscribers and promote one of your products or services that would be a good fit for them. There's an old saying, "people don't like to be sold, but they love to buy." When you educate your subscribers and let them know where they can find even more information or a solution to their problem, they will naturally buy from you without any hard selling required. As Zig Ziglar said, "if you help enough people get what they want in life, you can have everything you want in life." Focus on creating emails and content that help your subscribers solve their most important problems, and you will be handsomely rewarded.

Squeeze Page

A squeeze page is a web page where someone can opt-in to an email list. This specially designed page hosts a web form, and usually has no other active links or navigation options so that browsers can either choose to opt-in or leave the page. By limiting navigation options, a squeeze page will often convert 5x to 20x more than an opt-in form hosted on a blog or similar web page with many navigation options.

Here's an example of a squeeze page: www.BlogBusinessSchool.com See chapter 4 for more information on squeeze pages.

Conversion

A conversion is anytime someone converts from a visitor on your website or squeeze page to an email subscriber. A conversion could also be anytime someone converts from a visitor on your site to a customer. The definition of conversion will depend on your personal goals, and will probably vary from web page to web page.

For example, on a squeeze page, your conversion goal would be to generate a new email subscriber. On a sales page where you sell a book, video course, or other product or service, your conversion goal would be to generate a new order. Conversions are a very important business metric that you should be tracking with analytics.

Conversion Rate

Conversion rate is the percentage of visitors who achieve your conversion goal. For example, if 100 people visit your squeeze page and 35 opt-in to your email list, that page has a 35% conversion rate. All else being equal, the higher the conversion rate, the better.

Most squeeze pages convert between 10% and 50% of visitors. Rarely, online marketers may achieve a conversion rate higher than 50%. As a beginner, if you can achieve a 30% conversion rate, that's pretty good. Anything less than 30% probably needs work. The easiest way to improve conversion rates is through split testing (see below).

You can't know what your conversion rate is without data, and that data comes from your web analytics.

Deliverability Rate

Deliverability rate is the percentage of email subscribers who receive emails when you send them through your autoresponder. Ideally, your autoresponder would have a 100% deliverability rate. Anything over 99% is great. Anything less than 99% is not good.

Note: Deliverability rate, as used here, means that the email provider of your subscriber received the email. This does **not** mean that the customer saw your email or opened it. It simply means that the email was sent from your autoresponder to the customer's email server. The email could have been blocked by a spam filter, lost in the spam folder, or another folder, or deleted by the subscriber.

Analytics

Analytics or web analytics is data from your website that tells you how many visitors you had in the past and what actions those visitors have taken on your site. Depending on what analytics tool(s) you're using, you can get additional information such as: when the visitors visited your site, what country or location they were in, how long they spent on your site, what their gender and demographics are, whether they opted-in to your email list or bought a product, and much more.

Generally speaking, for a beginner, the most important analytics information is:

1) How many visitors did you have?
2) How many visitors converted into email subscribers (or customers)?

Without these two basic data points, you're flying blind. You need to know how many visitors you had and how many converted into email subscribers in order to track your conversion rate. And your conversion rate is a very important (crucial) metric to let you know how well your marketing campaigns are working.

Open Rate

The open rate is the percentage of email subscribers who open a particular email. The average open rate for email is around 26%, so if you beat the average you're doing well. Achieving a 40% or higher open rate is excellent.

Split Testing or A/B Testing

An A/B test is when you take two web pages (like two squeeze pages) and send traffic to both pages. You then use analytics to track traffic and conversions on both pages, and when you have enough data, keep the page that converts better and delete the other page. A split test is the same as an A/B test, although a split test could test more than two web pages at once.

Without split testing, it is highly unlikely that your website will ever achieve its full potential for converting visitors to email subscribers. A very small change in conversion rate due to split testing could increase your profits exponentially. Here's an example.

Let's say you run a split test and squeeze page A has a 30% conversion rate and squeeze page B has a 40% conversion rate. A 10% increase isn't a big deal, right? Actually, it's HUGE!

Even though it's only a 10% nominal increase in conversions, it's a 25% *relative* increase. This means you'll end up with 25% more email subscribers and, all else being equal, 25% more paying customers. That's a 25% increase in revenue for your business with just a simple split test.

This is why split testing is so important and so valuable. Using split testing, I personally took my average squeeze page conversion from about 20% to over 36%, with some of my pages converting as high as 56%. That's almost a doubling of my email subscribers *with the same amount of traffic*. In other words, I could spend the same amount of money now on traffic and get twice as many email subscribers (and twice as many paying customers) without any additional marketing expense. Without split testing, I could never have achieved that kind of increase in profitability. All successful online marketers use split tests to improve their websites and conversions.

Dollar-for-dollar, the best money you can spend as an email marketer is on split testing. That's why I highly recommend Leadpages (https://www.leadpages.net/) because it makes split testing so easy, fast and cost effective.

Landing Page

A landing page is the page that a visitor first sees when they visit a website. The landing page could be a squeeze page, home page, or any other page designated by the site owner depending on your particular marketing campaign and goals.

Generally speaking, you should always have a particular goal for your landing page. Typical goals for a landing page might include:

Getting the visitor to opt-in to your email list.
Getting the visitor to make a purchase.
Getting the visitor to fill out a contact form or inquiry form to request more information or schedule a phone call.
Getting the visitor to click on a link to buy a product from a third-party website or vendor (like Amazon.com to buy your book, for example).
Getting the visitor to call in to request more information or purchase on the phone.

Single Opt-in and Double Opt-in

Single opt-in is when a subscriber fills out your opt-in form and is immediately subscribed to your list. They only have to opt-in once.

A double opt-in is when a subscriber must click a link in an email after opting-in to your form in order to confirm their opt-in. This two-step process is called a double opt-in. First, they have to fill out the opt-in form on your site, and then they have to confirm again by clicking a confirmation link in an email.

There are benefits and drawbacks to each method.

For single opt-in, the benefits are you'll get more email subscribers, and you'll build your list faster. The downside is that you may get more fake emails, as well as potentially receive more spam complaints.

For double opt-in, the benefits are that you'll only have subscribers on your list who were committed enough to opt-in twice. Your list will be smaller but more focused with dedicated subscribers. Your autoresponder fees may be slightly lower because your list is smaller. You'll likely receive less spam complaints than someone using single opt-in.

Personally, I prefer single opt-in most of the time because it helps me grow a bigger list faster. However, many intelligent marketers choose double opt-in. You'll have to make your own choice as to what's best for you and your particular business.

Spam Complaint

A spam complaint is whenever someone reports your email as spam to your autoresponder service provider. It's normal to receive a few spam complaints here and there, but if you're receiving more than 1% or 2% spam complaints consistently, it's definitely not a good sign. If you get enough spam complaints, your autoresponder may give you a warning or even disable your account.

You can lower your spam complaints by writing clear, brief, and well-written emails, by using double opt-in instead of single opt-in, and by sending only relevant, targeted information to your subscribers. For example, if someone signs up for information about email marketing, don't send them information about potty training dogs. Keep your emails targeted and relevant to avoid spam complaints (that might sound obvious, but you'd be surprised what some email marketers will send to their list).

Also, pay attention to your traffic sources. Sometimes, traffic from the wrong place can increase your spam complaints. For example, if you're marketing a health product on a website for tech geeks, they might not even remember why they signed up for your list and why you're sending them health information. It's best to attract qualified traffic from sources that are reliable and in tune with your message and products.

Traffic

Traffic is a generic term for visitors or people who visit websites online. As an email marketer, you will need traffic to go to your squeeze page or other web pages so that they can opt-in to your email list.

The more traffic you get, the better, assuming that you have quality traffic.

Quality traffic means that your visitors are "targeted."

Targeted Traffic
Targeted traffic is quality traffic consisting of prospects that could buy from you. For example, if you sell a product only in the US, any visitor from outside the US would not be targeted traffic for your business because they cannot buy from you.

If you sell custom motorcycles and you're getting traffic from women age 45-65 who are into fashion, that's probably not targeted traffic because the demographic of those visitors doesn't match the demographic of your ideal customers. Not all traffic is the same!

You must understand that targeted traffic is what you want. It doesn't matter how *cheap* or *easy* it is to generate traffic: what matters is whether or not that traffic is targeted, and if they ultimately convert into customers for your business. Paying a little bit more for higher quality traffic is often worth it, and may end up saving you money because you'll be generating more revenue from higher quality leads.

This is why I *highly recommend* <u>never</u> paying for traffic from sites like Fiverr.com or any other website that promises cheap, quick or easy traffic. Cheap, quick and easy traffic is a myth. Real success in business takes work. The pros may make it look easy, but that's because they put the time, effort and energy into it to make it work. The only traffic I recommend buying is from a targeted, high quality source, the most common of which would be Pay Per Click (PPC) Ads.

Pay Per Click (PPC) Advertising
PPC advertising is an online advertising model where you pay each time a visitor clicks the link to your website in the ad. The two biggest PPC advertising platforms are Facebook Ads and Google Adwords.

Most email marketers right now prefer Facebook Ads for building an email list because it's easier to learn how to use and often cheaper for many markets.

You do not need to use PPC advertising to build an email list. It's just one potential method for generating traffic to build your list.

CHAPTER 2

THE MINDSET OF AN EMAIL SUBSCRIBER

Before we delve into the steps to start building your email list, it's important to understand the mindset of an email subscriber so that you can understand the potential (and limitations) of email marketing.

WHY WOULD SOMEONE SIGN UP FOR AN EMAIL LIST ANYWAY?
Today, it's become common practice for email marketers to offer a free gift in exchange for someone opting in to their email list. So, many email subscribers sign up for a list because they want the free gift being offered.

Here are some common free gifts you could give away to start building your email list:

A free report (usually a multi-page PDF report on a specific topic).

A free cheat sheet (usually a one- or two-page downloadable PDF that is useful to your prospect, such as a checklist or goal-setting worksheet).

A free video (an educational video that shows your prospect how to do something).

A free audio file (an educational audio that shows your prospect how to do something. Sometimes, an interview with a celebrity or leader in your field).

A webinar (a live or recorded online video/audio training session where you teach your subscriber something valuable, and may or may not offer an additional product or service to the webinar attendees at the end).

I highly recommend only offering a free gift that is automated. For example, I would not recommend offering a free 30-minute strategy session on the phone with you, because that will place constraints on how fast and how large you can build your email list. You will simply run out of time when your schedule is full of strategy sessions, and would no longer be able to deliver the free gift you promised to your email subscribers. There are definitely times when you may want to offer a free 30-minute strategy session in order to build a deeper relationship with your customers and offer them a chance to buy your higher-end products or services, but I would not recommend it for your first free offer to build your email list. Choose a free gift that you can automate, so that you can spend time growing your list and helping your subscribers solve their problems.

In my experience, a free downloadable PDF report will provide the highest conversion rate most of the time, so if you're not sure what to offer, start with a free downloadable report.

WHAT DO SUBSCRIBERS REALLY WANT?
There are two main types of email subscribers: fans and solution seekers.

Fans are people who know you, like you and just want to stay connected with you through your email list. They may not want anything specific from you other than a social connection, but often the best fans want to buy every product or service you offer because they like you so much and resonate with your message. For example, if you're a novelist or author and readers love your book, you might want to add a link to your squeeze page inside your books so that your fans can subscribe and stay up to date on your newest books and work.

If you already have fans but they're not on your email list yet, ask them to sign up!

Solution seekers are people with a problem, and they're looking for a solution. They may not even know you or like you yet, but they have a problem, and they think you may know how to help them solve it. For example, if you're reading this book, you may have a problem: you want to grow your business using email marketing, but you're not sure how to do it. In this book, I'll show you how to solve that problem. You may have never heard of me before buying this book, and that's okay. Remember, the purpose of a business is to solve problems for people. Most businesses will attract a lot of solution seekers who are looking for your solution to their problem.

Understanding which kind of subscribers you have (most email marketers will have both, but in different proportions) will help you understand what kinds of emails to send to your list to maximize sales.

For example, if you immediately send a sales pitch to a list of solution seekers who are not fans, your conversion rate will likely be very low, and you may find a lot of subscribers get turned off by the sales pitch and unsubscribe. Instead, you should send one or several educational emails to solution seekers in order to build a deeper relationship with them. By adding more value up front before asking them to buy something, you are building stronger rapport and you will be able to convert some of these people who had never heard of you before into customers and maybe even raving fans.

If your list is full of fans, you probably don't need to warm them up before sending a sales pitch. If you're a novelist and every one of your email subscribers has read at least one of your books before, simply sending an email announcing your newest book release will do just fine. It's highly unlikely you will turn anyone off with an honest, direct offer when they are already fans. Sending an offer or sales pitch to an email list of fans will often generate higher conversion than an offer sent to a list of solution seekers, because fans trust you more. The more trust there is, the faster sales will happen.

BOTH IS BETTER

The best email subscribers you can get are both fans and solution seekers. They love you and what you do, and they have a problem that you can help them solve through your products or services. These subscribers will tend to buy everything you offer and share your message with others, and share a testimonial as well of how you helped them so much. These are your raving fan customers, and they are incredibly valuable and important for a business. One raving fan customer can bring in dozens of new clients through word of mouth. You can create more raving fan customers more quickly by understanding who your current followers are and what they're looking for from your business.

For example, if you're a novelist and have a lot of fans, you might want to try to convert your fans into solution seekers. What problems might your fans have that you could help them solve? You could create a Facebook group or online community where all of your fans can connect and discuss your books and other topics. This community can help bond your fans together and add more value to them. In return, your fans will be more loyal, more educated, and more likely to share your message with non-fans.

If you have a lot of solution seekers and little or no fans, you'll want to try to turn your solution seekers into fans. You can do this by getting really good at helping your subscribers solve their problems. You can use surveys, phone calls, and do research to find out more about what your subscribers want and how best to help them. You can offer free video trainings, webinars, and educational events where you give massive amounts of value to them. You can offer coaching calls to connect with your audience one-on-one to really dive deep into their problems and provide even more effective solutions. The more value you add to your subscribers, the more they will appreciate and like you. Turning solution seekers into fans is how internet marketing giants like Frank Kern and Brendon Burchard became so popular. They have raving fans who love their products, buy all their products, and tell lots of other people about

15

them. One raving fan can do more to help grow your business than 100 lukewarm customers.

Understand Your Subscribers

Your goal should be to understand your subscribers. The better you understand them – their problems and what they want – the better you can help them get what they want, and the faster your business will grow.

Use surveys, phone calls, and live events to connect with your audience and learn more about them. You can also research forums online where your ideal customers hang out and listen to what problems, challenges, hopes and dreams your ideal customers have. Then, use that information to create better products, services and helpful tools and information to help your customers even more. Don't just stay locked away in your office every day. Get out and connect with your audience on a personal level.

The more value you add to your subscribers and prospects, the more subscribers and customers you will attract.

At the end of the day, the better you understand your subscribers and customers, the more profitable your business will be. Invest the time, money and energy necessary to get to know your audience. It's one of the best investments you can make.

CHAPTER 3
ELEVEN STEPS TO BUILDING AN EMAIL LIST

STEP 1. GET AN AUTORESPONDER

Your autoresponder is your key software system that manages your email list for you. It's important you choose one that is reliable, and learn to use it as best you can.

FREE AUTORESPONDERS

www.Launchrock.com
Right now, I believe Launchrock is the best free autoresponder. It's easy to use and setup, has good deliverability rates, and uses well-designed squeeze page and opt-in form templates (meaning you'll have higher conversion rates than you would get with poorly-designed templates.)

www.Mailchimp.com
Mailchimp is a commonly used free autoresponder, but I don't like it because of it's poorly designed templates and low deliverability rates. Furthermore, in my experience working with clients, converting your list from Mailchimp to another autoresponder service is difficult and often results in a huge loss of subscribers (which is not good.)

PAID AUTORESPONDERS

All of the paid autoresponders listed below are better and more reliable than the free autoresponders. Therefore, if you have a budget of \$15 a month, definitely upgrade to one of these paid autoresponders. You'll earn a lot more in the long run and save yourself a lot of hassles.

www.GetResponse.com
Many marketers consider GetResponse to be the best low-budget autoresponder right now. It's very well designed, has excellent deliverability rates, and their templates are fantastic. It also has very good analytics.

www.aweber.com
I use Aweber because that's the autoresponder I started with years ago, but if I were starting fresh today, I would choose GetResponse instead. Aweber has great deliverability, but GetResponse has better designed templates and opt-in forms.

www.Infusionsoft.com
Infusionsoft is a high-end autoresponder that has incredibly advanced CRM (Customer Relationship Management) capabilities, includes a shopping cart system, affiliate management, and much more. It starts at around \$299 a month, so it's definitely a high-end product. When creating sophisticated marketing funnels, Infusionsoft really stands out with its advanced features such as tagging subscribers, which allows you to tag every subscriber based on their interests or what web pages they clicked on in the past. You can then use these tags and set up automation systems to transfer subscribers to more targeted lists based on what they want and how they have interacted with your business so far.

OTHER AUTORESPONDERS
There are many, many more autoresponders, but I don't have personal experience working with them all, so I've only covered the ones I recommend most in this book.

Step 2. Create an Opt-In Form (Web Form)

Once you have your autoresponder, it's time to use it to build an opt-in form so that people can sign up for your email list.

Every autoresponder has a slightly different site layout and system for creating opt-in forms, but they all have the same basic components:

Designing Your Web Form

Your autoresponder should have its own custom design tool for web forms. With the opt-in form design tool that comes with your autoresponder, you should be able to change the text size, color, fonts, and other features of your web form. If you're not a good designer and need a great-looking web form to match your site, you can hire a designer to create one for you. You can hire someone on Fiverr.com for just $5 to create a custom web form design for you based on your needs.

Thank You Page Link (Confirmation Page Link)

When you create your web form, you should set up a redirect to a custom thank you page link. On the thank you page, you should thank your subscribers for joining your list and provide them with a way to download or access your free report or free offer that you promised.

Every autoresponder will have a pre-built thank you page that is generic and branded for your autoresponder. I don't recommend using the generic thank you page unless you're just starting out. You will need a web designer or a service like LeadPages to create your custom thank you page. You can always go back and change your web form design and settings later, so if you are brand new to email marketing, just set it up and make sure it's working. Don't put off creating your email list system until you have every single thing figured out. Much of it you will learn as you go and as you implement the steps in this book.

ALREADY SUBSCRIBED PAGE LINK

Any person who is already subscribed to your email list who fills out your web form will be redirected to the already subscribed page. I normally just keep this page the same as my thank you page, because I figure if a subscriber is going to fill out the form a second time, they must have missed the free download the first time.

CREATING YOUR WEB FORM VIDEO TUTORIAL

There is a short video that walks you through the process step-by-step for creating a web form with Aweber. You can watch it for free on YouTube at https://www.youtube.com/watch?v=Z-tQzaom3TY

If you decide to use another autoresponder service, don't worry. It's the same process you'll be going through to create your opt-in form. The only difference is the buttons will be in different places on the page, and other autoresponders may offer slightly different features. All the key features will be the same: you will have to design your web form and choose a thank you page and an already subscribed page before you can install your web form on your site.

If you're using a different autoresponder and don't know how to create your opt-in form, check the help forum inside your autoresponder account for a tutorial and/or call or email your autoresponder's customer support staff and they will show you how to do it quickly and easily. All of the autoresponder services mentioned in this book have tutorials and instructional guides on these basic steps, and they have a responsive support team that will answer your questions and give you guidance if you get stuck. Remember, they don't make money if their customers don't know how to use their service! So they're highly incentivized to help teach you if you get stuck trying to set up your opt-in forms or email marketing systems.

Note: I always recommend buying software solutions from a company with phone support, because it can save you a lot of time and money if you run into a problem you don't know how to solve. A good phone support team can help you solve your problems a lot faster and prevent lost revenue and profits from a technical problem. Even if you have to pay a little more to get phone support, it's definitely worth it in my experience. Trying to figure out everything on your own can sometimes end up being a big waste of time and money! Having great phone support is like having another employee on your staff who can help you solve problems and make progress without costing you a dime. When in doubt, call for backup so that you can get your problems solved as fast as possible.

STEP 3. CREATE A WEB PAGE TO HOST YOUR OPT-IN FORM ON
Don't worry if you don't have a web page and don't know how to build a website. Every good autoresponder will host your web form for you on their website. This isn't always the best option for you in terms of maximizing your conversions, but it's free and/or included in the price of your autoresponder. It usually just takes one click to set it up, so you don't need to understand HTML or coding or any fancy technical terms. If you are a complete beginner to online marketing, you can start by having your opt-in form hosted on your autoresponder's site for free.

If you have a budget of $37 a month or more, Leadpages (https://www.leadpages.net/) is by far the best service I've found to create squeeze pages and landing pages that convert well. We will discuss LeadPages in more detail later in this book.

If you already have your own blog or website, you can install your opt-in form on your existing site.

Note: If you're using a free blog hosted on wordpress.com such as example.wordpress.com, you will NOT be able to install a web form on your site. You will need to create a self-hosted site that you own and control completely. If you have no idea how to do that yet, you can watch the free training videos at www. BlogBusinessSchool.com.

STEP 4. CHOOSE SINGLE OPT-IN OR DOUBLE OPT-IN

If you choose double opt-in, you'll need an extra web page, usually called a confirmation page, that asks your subscriber to confirm their information.

If you're not sure how to choose single opt-in or double opt-in with your particular autoresponder, email or call their customer support team and they can walk you through the process.

If you're not sure what the difference is between single and double opt-in, refer to the Email Marketing Definitions section.

STEP 5. CREATE A GIFT OR DELIVERABLE (OPTIONAL BUT HIGHLY RECOMMENDED)

After someone opts-in to your email list, you'll need to deliver what you promised. If you promised a free report or video training, give it to them right away on the thank you page.

Make it easy and fast for them to access the information you promised. A simple link to the download page or video page works great, or you can just set your autoresponder to automatically forward the subscriber directly to the page where your content is delivered.

STEP 6. SET UP A THANK YOU PAGE

Your thank you page delivers your gift, thanks the customer, and/ or provides instructions for the next steps your subscriber should take. All autoresponders will have a standard thank you page. This is generally a poor choice. Instead, you'll want to create your own custom thank you page. If you use Wordpress, you can simply create your own thank you page that has a link to your free report or gift.

If you use Leadpages, you can create a custom thank you page and use split testing to track conversions on your thank you page.

You can also offer a product or service for sale as well on your thank you page. For example, on your page you could link to your free report, and then underneath that, write something like:

"Hey, if you like this free report on email marketing, then you'll love my complete email marketing video course. Click here to learn more."

See a Thank You Page in Action

Here's an example of a thank you page that converted very well for a promotion we did for the 20 Life-Changing Books Box Set: https://tckpublishing.leadpages.net/sweepstakes-thank-you-page/

Step 7. Write Your Autoresponder Series

Next, you'll want to write your autoresponder series that will help you build a closer relationship with your subscribers, educate them, and offer them more relevant products or services to buy.

In your first autoresponder email (the welcome email), make sure to include a link to your free gift in case the subscriber missed it on your thank you page. You might want to give them a brief preview of what to expect as well in future emails. For example, you could write something like this:

"Stay tuned for future updates where I'll share with you how I went from 0 to over $12,000+ a month in Kindle ebook royalties in just 12 months."

Of course, don't make claims unless they're true. And make sure to talk to your attorney about when, where, why and how to use legal disclaimers in your marketing material.

Step 8. Test Your System

Once you've completed steps 1-7, it's time to start testing your system. Sign up for your email list yourself and go through all the steps that your subscribers will have to go through to get on your email list. Make sure the opt-in form works, check every page and step of the process and make sure that every link, button and web page is working properly before you start sending traffic to your new opt-in page.

This will help avoid any problems or disappointed subscribers. Nothing will turn people off faster than a broken opt-in form, or not delivering what you promised you would deliver when someone signs up for your email list.

You should also test all your web pages on different web browsers (like Chrome, Firefox, Internet Explorer and Safari), as well as on mobile devices (like an iPhone and iPad) to make sure your system will work for anyone regardless of what device or web browser they use.

Here's what you should test every time you set up a new autoresponder series to make sure every page and step in your email marketing system is working as planned:

1) Test the web form
2) Test the confirmation page (if you use double opt-in)
3) Test the confirmation email (if you use double opt-in)
4) Test the thank you page
5) Test all links on your thank you page
6) Test all links and proofread your Autoresponder welcome email and any other autoresponder emails
7) Test your already subscribed page (fill out your opt-in form twice in a row with the same email address, and make sure the second time you fill it out, you are taken to the correct page for people who are already subscribed page).
8) Test steps 1-7 on every major web browser (Internet Explorer, Mozilla Firefox, Google Chrome, Safari) and on mobile devices (iPhone, Android and iPad).

STEP 9. GETTING TRAFFIC

Now that you've created your email marketing system and tested it, it's time to send traffic to your web page with your opt-in form to get subscribers.

As a general rule of thumb, you should always be linking to your squeeze page in every piece of content you put out online. You'll probably want to link to your squeeze page in your email signature, and in every blog post, article, video and any other piece of content you create. The more links to your squeeze page, the more traffic you will get. This is called "free traffic" because you're not paying for it. If someone finds your video on YouTube and then goes to your squeeze page, that's "free" traffic because you didn't pay for it.

If you use PPC advertising, that's called paid traffic because you're paying for clicks.

Online marketers who are trying to sell you a product will often say that their method of getting traffic and subscribers is the best. But there is no one best method for building your email list. You should try as many methods as you can (and can afford), and focus on the methods that give you the highest long-term return on investment (ROI).

In my personal experience, free traffic from my own content provides the highest long-term return on investment. When I create educational videos, blog posts, podcast shows, and other educational content, I'm attracting solution seekers and fans who then sign up for my email list. This free traffic is great because I'm attracting highly targeted subscribers, and the long-term ROI is huge because the cost of creating educational content is so low (and in many cases doesn't cost anything but time).

STEP 10. SEND BROADCAST EMAILS
Once you've built up your email list and your subscribers have gone through your autoresponder series, it's time to start sending relevant broadcast emails to further educate, entertain and market to your email list.

A broadcast email is like a normal email you would send to a friend, except it only goes out to your email list. Unlike regular emails, you can schedule a broadcast to be sent anytime in the future, or you can send the broadcast email immediately after writing it.

Broadcast emails are what you will usually use to promote a new book or product launch, make an announcement, or just send out a timely one-time update to your email list.

STEP 11. IMPLEMENT ANALYTICS AND CONVERSION TRACKING
In this final step, we're going to cover analytics and conversions and learn about some awesome tools, systems and strategies for increasing your conversions so that you can build a bigger, more profitable email list even faster.

WHY YOU NEED ANALYTICS
Trying to build a business without analytics is like trying to play pin the tail on the donkey blindfolded. Sure, it's fun, but you're going to miss more often than you hit, and your chances of success are slim.

Using analytics and split testing can turn an unprofitable business into a soaring, profitable business in just a few months. There's an old saying in advertising and marketing that half of your marketing budget is being wasted, but no one knows which half. Thanks to modern analytics and conversion tracking, the marketing and advertising world has changed. Today, if you're wasting half your marketing budget, that is entirely your fault for not setting up proper analytics and conversion tracking for your business.

With good analytics, you can see very quickly whether your marketing dollars are working for you or not. This means you can shut down unprofitable marketing campaigns faster, test new campaigns, and scale up profitable campaigns more easily. Have you ever wondered why it seems like so many entrepreneurs and businesses are going from zero to millions of dollars in sales online so quickly?

Good analytics is why. When a business uses analytics properly, it can achieve a 2x, 3x and even a 10x faster growth rate profitably by eliminating unprofitable marketing campaigns and scaling up profitable campaigns in a fraction of the time it used to take. Good marketing is about good decision making. It's a lot easier to make good decisions when you have the right data.

Great analytics data (and the knowledge it takes to interpret that data) can turn a struggling business into a super-profitable growth machine. Is there more to growing a business than just having good analytics? Absolutely. But most entrepreneurs already know they need to create great products and connect with customers on a deeper level. In my experience, one of the biggest mistakes new online entrepreneurs make is not properly using analytics to help them make better marketing decisions.

LIFETIME VALUE OF A CUSTOMER (LTV)

The Lifetime Value of a Customer (LTV) is the total direct dollar value a customer brings to your business. For example, if the average customer buys a $100 product from you every year for five years, the LTV of that customer is $500 (before discounting the cash flow).

If you know the LTV of your customers, then you know how much you can afford to spend to attract a new customer. If your LTV is $500, you can spend up to $500 to attract a new customer and still make a profit. If you spend more, you're losing money on your marketing.

Until you really understand the LTV of your customers, it's hard to make good marketing decisions because you won't know how much you can afford to spend to attract a new customer while still making a profit.

Note: LTV does not take into account indirect revenue from a customer, such as revenue from that customer referring other customers to your business. For this reason, and because of network effects and the additional value that growth provides for a business, there are some cases where a business owner would be wise to spend more money on bringing in a new customer than the LTV. For example, if you spend $600 to attract a new customer with an LTV of $500 and that customer refers another customer with an LTV of $500, the business enjoys $400 in profit by "overspending" on marketing.

GOOGLE ANALYTICS

Google Analytics is free, and it's one of the most commonly used and most powerful analytics tools. You can sign up for Google Analytics at www.google.com/analytics

Google Analytics can provide detailed analytics on visitors to any website you own. To install Google Analytics on your website, you will either need to understand a little bit of coding, hire a web designer to help, or use Wordpress with a free plugin like Google Analytics for WordPress at https://wordpress.org/plugins/google-analytics-for-wordpress/

HEAT MAPS

www.Crazyegg.com provides heat maps and analytics for your site. A heat map is basically a visual image of your website that lights up every time a visitor clicks somewhere on your site. This heat map allows you to see where users are clicking on your website. This information can help you increase your conversions and create a better website by putting links to higher-converting web pages and offers where your visitors tend to click the most.

LEADPAGES

Leadpages provides basic analytics that track visitors and conversions. Again, I highly recommend Leadpages because it makes creating squeeze pages, sales pages, thank you pages, and other key landing pages incredibly easy. It also allows you to do unlimited split testing so that you can increase your conversion rates over time by testing what works and what doesn't work. To hire a web designer to do what Leadpages can do for you, it would easily cost you hundreds or thousands of dollars a month.

WHEN POSSIBLE, ALWAYS USE MORE ANALYTICS

In nature, there is a powerful principle called redundancy. For example, humans have two kidneys and two eyes. We don't need two of them. We can survive just fine with one eye or one kidney, but we have two. This is redundancy – having more than you need. The reason redundancy is such a powerful survival tool in nature is that you can lose one and still function and survive. If you have one kidney and lose it, you're dead. If you have two kidneys and lose one, you're okay. Little backup mechanisms like that have helped life thrive here on Earth despite huge changes over millions of years.

Likewise in business, if you have two analytics tools, and one stops working, you're okay. If you have only one tool and it stops working, your business is at risk because you no longer have the data you need to make better marketing decisions.

When possible, always have redundancy built in to your business. This is why you'll want to back up your email list, websites and any key business documents more than once. In case something bad happens and you lose all your data, you'll always have multiple backups in place.

Don't let one little mistake ruin your business. Always have multiple backups and implement redundancy whenever possible.

CHAPTER 4
USING SQUEEZE PAGES TO BUILD YOUR LIST FASTER

A squeeze page is a web page that basically gives visitors two options: either they can sign up for your email list or they can leave the page.

There are usually no navigation bars or outbound links on a squeeze page, and nothing extra to distract visitors from the main goal of the page: to opt-in to the email list in return for your free offer.

Squeeze pages are by far the most effective type of web pages for building your email list. The conversion rate on a squeeze page will usually be 5x to 20x better than the conversion rate on a typical blog or website with an opt-in form. A good blog with an opt-in box on the top right usually converts around 1-4% whereas a squeeze page often converts anywhere from 10% to 40% or more. Therefore, whenever possible, and when it makes sense for your business, send traffic to your squeeze page and not your blog, so that you can build your list faster.

How to Build a Squeeze Page
My favorite way to build a squeeze page is with Leadpages because it's fast, easy, and you can immediately start tracking conversions and set up a split test to improve your results.

Building a Free Squeeze Page with Wordpress
There are some Wordpress plugins that allow you to build a squeeze page for free.

One free option is WP Lead Plus Free Squeeze Pages Creator: https://wordpress.org/plugins/wp-lead-plus-free-squeeze-pages-creator

If you're on a tight budget, starting with a free squeeze page using a free Wordpress plugin is probably your best bet. If you plan to spend more than $250 a month to build your email list, you should definitely get LeadPages because it will help you get much better results from your marketing budget.

CHAPTER 5

BUILDING YOUR LIST AND GETTING TRAFFIC

Despite what some cheesy online marketers selling push-button software may say, email lists don't just build themselves.

There are many, many ways to get traffic and build your email list. To be successful with email marketing, you have to generate plenty of traffic. And targeted traffic is what you're looking for. Traffic that isn't targeted could actually be damaging to your business (by wasting time, money and resources on visitors who could never become paying customers.)

In this section, we'll cover some of the most common and effective strategies for creating traffic in order to build your email list.

CONVERTING A LIST OF CONTACTS INTO EMAIL LIST SUBSCRIBERS

If you already have subscribers whom you have been sending informal emails to without an autoresponder, you should add your list of contacts into your autoresponder. But first, a few words of caution:

Never add anyone to your email list unless they have asked to be added. If you have been sending emails to random people who may not even know who you are and don't want to receive emails from you, do NOT add them to your autoresponder.

If your autoresponder requires them to confirm to opt-in, they won't confirm. And if your autoresponder does not require confirmation, your new email subscribers will likely report you for spamming which can have serious consequences.

If you have a list of contacts you have been emailing in the past without an autoresponder, I would send them one final email and let them know that you are moving to a professional email marketing system or email newsletter system, and tell them that they will have to confirm in order to receive your newsletter in the future.

Let them know that if they do not confirm, they will not be receiving any further emails from you.

It's better to play it safe and do things right than try to get a few more email subscribers by adding people to your list who aren't actually interested. Getting lots of spam complaints and angry subscribers is not good for business. You need targeted traffic and happy subscribers to keep your business growing.

BLOGGING

The most common and simple way to start building your email list is with a blog. Once you've installed your opt-in forms on your blog, you'll start to get new subscribers to your list. In my experience, opt-in forms placed at the top right of a blog usually convert between 1%-4% of visitors. So, if you get 100 visitors to your blog, one to four of them will sign up for your email list, assuming you have a good offer and targeted traffic.

VIDEO MARKETING

If you create educational videos or post videos on YouTube, you can use those videos to start building your email list.

I love video marketing for building my email list because it's a long-term strategy that consistently outperforms just about every other method for email list building in terms of time commitment. A helpful, educational or entertaining 5-minute video could create hundreds or even thousands of new email subscribers over the next five to ten years.

In my experience, a YouTube video with a link to an email opt-in page usually converts anywhere from 0.1% to 1% of viewers. In other words, you'll get a new email subscriber for every 100 to 1,000 views on YouTube (assuming you have a video and offer that are targeted to your specific audience).

YouTube Marketing Tip: Put the link to your squeeze page in the first line of every YouTube video. Make sure to include "http://" before the link and test it by clicking the link to make sure it works properly.

Public Speaking

Public speaking is a great way to build your email list. If you offer a product or service for sale when you speak publicly, you can also have your buyers opt-in to your email newsletter. If you're not selling anything during your speech, you can create a giveaway for anyone who signs up for your email list, or offer a free report or other free offer in exchange for collecting emails from your audience. If you are a frequent public speaker and you are not currently either selling a product or service or building your email list when you speak, you are missing out on a HUGE opportunity to grow your email list and your business through public speaking.

Media

If you're doing TV or radio interviews, the best way to start building your email list is by making it easy for your listeners or viewers to get your free offer. The best way to do this is by using a forwarded domain to your squeeze page.

For example, it's a lot easier to say on air "Go to EbookPublishingSchool.com to sign up for your free training" instead of "Go to EbookPublishingSchool.com/free-offer-that's-really-hard-to-remember."

The shorter and easier it is to remember the domain you ask listeners to go to, the more people will actually sign up for your email list. Keep it short, simple and easy to remember. If you say your domain out loud, someone should immediately understand exactly how to spell your domain and find it online. Avoid puns and ambiguous language or words with homophones if possible to avoid confusing listeners and sending them to the wrong website. If you have the budget, you can also buy commonly misspelled versions of your website. For example, you could buy "business.com" and "busines.com" and forward them to your main domain. That way, if someone types in a misspelling of your website in their web browser, they are still sent directly to your website instead of a competitor's site or a Google search page.

PAY PER CLICK (PPC) ADS

There are many, many PPC advertising platforms, but the biggest are Facebook Ads and Google Adwords. Most online marketers prefer Facebook Ads for email list building because of Facebook's highly advanced targeting based on user interests.

If you're going to use PPC advertising, you should definitely consider getting Leadpages (https://www.leadpages.net/) so that you can run split tests quickly and easily to increase your conversions. Using PPC ads without detailed analytics and split testing will most likely be unprofitable, time-consuming and waste a lot of your money.

If you're going to start PPC advertising and have no experience doing it before, definitely get Leadpages or a similar split testing system. Most PPC campaigns are unprofitable at first until you run multiple split tests and start improving your conversions. Start with a small budget, run split tests, and continue testing until you find the right ads and landing pages that create the highest profit for your business.

Be willing to invest 6-12 months and several thousand dollars with at least 10 split tests to create a profitable PPC campaign. Yes, some marketers have created profitable campaigns in less time with less money and less split tests, but you should not count on it. It's better to be safe than sorry. Give yourself room to make mistakes, learn and improve over time. The more split tests you run, the more profitable your business will become over time. With 10 split tests, you should be able to increase your conversions by 50% or more, which should mean a 50% or greater increase in profits.

Email Signature

Create a custom email signature that links to your squeeze page, blog and/or sales page. Every time you send an email, it should provide a link to your websites. This can turn your every-day emails into marketing and lead generation opportunities without any additional work once you set up your email signature.

CHAPTER 6
FREE, LOW COST AND HIGH-END EMAIL MARKETING SOLUTIONS

FREE AND LOW BUDGET EMAIL MARKETING OPTIONS
Launchrock (free)
Mailchimp: http://mailchimp.com/ (free)
Sendy.co: https://sendy.co/ (cheap one-time payment)
Amazon SES: https://aws.amazon.com/ses/ (incredibly cheap)
Blogger blog: https://www.blogger.com/about/?r=1-null_user (free)
Tumblr blog: https://www.tumblr.com/ (free)

PREMIUM OPTIONS AND THE BEST TOOLS
GetResponse: https://www.getresponse.com/ (starting at $15/m)
Aweber: http://www.aweber.com/home.htm (starting at $29/m)
Infusionsoft: https://www.infusionsoft.com/ (starting at $299/m)

LEADPAGES: HTTPS://WWW.LEADPAGES.NET/ (STARTING AT $37/M)
If you've got a small email marketing budget, I *highly* recommend getting Leadpages. I'm not a tech expert, coder or web programmer. I only know a tiny bit of HTML. The great thing about Leadpages is that with absolutely no coding experience, you can design world-class, professional, customized opt-in pages and sales pages in just a few minutes.

You can also use split testing and get detailed analytics for all your opt-in pages and sales pages using Leadpages.

Leadpages syncs with Wordpress, so it's super easy to use if you have an existing Wordpress site. You can just download their Wordpress plugin which is included with your membership, and with the click of a button you can install your custom Leadpages on your own Wordpress site and start capturing leads and running split tests right away. You don't even need to own your own website to start using Leadpages to build your list.

You also have the option to host your Leadpages sites on their hosting platform which has lightning-fast load speed and 24/7 uptime (so you can convert more leads, and you don't need to pay for hosting or worry about missing leads if your site goes down temporarily.)

Leadpages starts at $37 a month, but you don't get their split testing options unless you go for the premium package at $67 a month. I recommend getting the $67 a month package so that you can start running split tests and improve your conversion rates. If you plan on spending more than $250 a month on traffic to build your email list, you'll end up saving money and dramatically increasing your profits by using Leadpages for split tests. You can also get a discount by upgrading to an annual subscription.

You can sign up for Leadpages here: https://www.leadpages.net/

SELF HOSTED WORDPRESS BLOG (VERY CHEAP AND **HIGHLY** RECOMMENDED)

I've created an entire free training course on how to build your own custom website using Wordpress. You can get access to the entire video training course at www.BlogBusinessSchool.com

It's very important that you *own* your website or blog. In order for that to happen, you must own your domain name and purchase web hosting (there are free web hosting services, but I wouldn't recommend any of them.)

If your blog is hosted on Blogger (example.blogger.com), Wordpress (example.wordpress.com), Tumblr (example.tumblr.com) or any other 3rd-party domain, *you do not own your website.* That company owns your website. That means 1) you do not have complete control over your site, 2) you could lose your entire site at any time, and 3) you may not be able to install opt-in forms or sell products or services effectively on your site.

As I'm writing this book, Blogger.com and Tumblr.com allow you to host an opt-in form on their free sites, but Wordpress.com does not.

Creating a custom site that you own using your own domain, your own web hosting, and Wordpress software, however, will give you complete control and ownership of your website. You can learn more at www.BlogBusinessSchool.com

CHAPTER 7
WRITING AND SENDING EMAILS TO YOUR LIST

There are two main types of emails you can send to your list with an autoresponder: broadcasts and autoresponders.

Broadcasts are spontaneous, one-time emails you can send to your subscribers. Broadcasts are just like any regular email you've sent in the past. You write it now, you send it now, and your subscribers receive the email right away.

Any good autoresponder will also allow you to schedule a broadcast to be delivered in the future. For example, you could write a broadcast email right now about your big launch coming up next weekend, and then tell your autoresponder to send the email to your list next weekend at a specific date and time. This is a great way to plan ahead and prepare for big launches and promotions ahead of time.

Autoresponders are emails that you write ahead of time and are delivered to your email subscribers based on when they sign up for your email list and when you want them to receive those pre-written emails.

You can use a series of autoresponder emails to drip-feed information to your subscribers on a regular schedule once they sign up for your list or deliver a series of informational emails, training videos, and other content.

BROADCASTS
Use broadcast emails when you're promoting something new or sending a one-time message or offer that is time-specific.

SUBJECT LINES

The subject line of your email is one of the most crucial pieces that will determine how many of your subscribers open your email. If they don't open your email, you can't build a relationship with them or sell anything. Subject lines are incredibly important. A good subject line is the first step in getting your email to make an impact.

Email marketers have different views on what the subject line should do, but virtually all agree that the main purpose of the subject line is just to get your subscribers to open the email. It doesn't have to be funny, cute or unique. It just has to work.

Here's the basic process you want your email subscribers to go through when you send an email.

1) Read the subject line
2) Open the email
3) Read the email
4) Click the link
5) Take your intended action (consume information, share, buy, etc.)

If you don't get past step 1, nothing good happens. That's why subject lines are so important.

Think of your email subject line like the headline of an advertisement or newspaper. It has to capture your audience's attention and get them to want to read more.

SUBJECT LINES AND SPAM FILTERS

Many spam filters will flag emails with certain words in the subject line. The list of words that are often flagged by spam filters is enormous. Here's just a sample of some commonly flagged words that you should avoid, or use very sparingly in your email subject lines:

Buy
Clearance
Additional income

Double your
Earn $
Make $
Money Making
Opportunity
Bargain
Affordable
No cost
Money back
No investment
Ad
Click
Open
Opt in
Sale
#1
4U
Million
Billion

Here are some links to much bigger lists of potential words that could get your emails stuck in spam filters:

http://blog.hubspot.com/blog/tabid/6307/bid/30684/
The-Ultimate-List-of-Email-SPAM-Trigger-Words.aspx
http://emailmarketing.comm100.com/email-marketing-
ebook/spam-words.aspx

SPLIT TESTING EMAILS AND SUBJECT LINES
Most autoresponders have a split testing function where you can split test your subject lines and email copy. If you're going to start split testing emails, I highly recommend starting by split testing subject lines. When you do a split test for a broadcast email, half of your list will get the email with subject line A and half will get the email with subject line B.

Once the emails have been sent, you'll get analytics and data on both groups and you can see which subject line produced more opens and clicks. If you see a big difference in opens between one subject line and another, write down the better performing subject line and keep it in a notebook or journal. These proven-to-work subject lines can be used for book titles, blog headlines, sales copy, and much more. If a subject line is proven to get people to open your emails better than other subject lines, then those same words will likely perform well with your audience as a headline, title, or other promotional text in another marketing campaign or project. The better data you have about what your audience likes and responds to, the better your marketing will become over time.

Keep a list of your best subject lines for later use. Many marketers sell or give away "swipe files" with headlines, subject lines and other marketing text that has performed well in the past. But the best swipe file you can get your hands on is the one you create that's proven to work for you with your particular audience.

Font Size

Most autoresponders default to size 12 font for messages. This is fine for most people, but subscribers with glasses or trouble seeing may find it difficult to read fonts at that size. I recommend using font size 14 for all your emails so that your subscribers can actually read them (it'll also save you a lot of time because you won't be getting emails from your subscribers complaining that it's difficult to read your emails.)

Email Spacing for Mobile

Most emails are now read on mobile devices which have smaller screens. For this reason, it's important to optimize the width of your emails so that all your subscribers can easily read them. If your emails are too wide, mobile readers will have to scroll left to right as well as down to read your email, which will be annoying for them and decrease your click-through rates.

The ideal pixel width for your email template should be between 320 and 500 pixels.

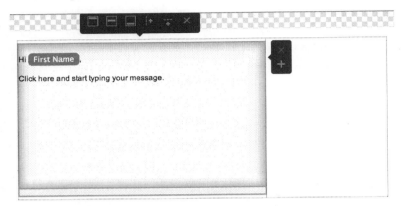

Above is a screenshot in Aweber of modifying the email width. Aweber calls this option "Vertical Split." Clicking the Vertical Split button once will reduce the width of the email to the ideal width for mobile devices.

If you're not sure how to adjust the width of your emails with your particular autoresponder, email or call their support team and they can give you detailed instructions.

CREATING EMAIL TEMPLATES

You should be able to create a template inside your autoresponder. You can set the template to 14 point font size and the ideal width for mobile devices, and then you can just load the template each time you write an email instead of having to make these adjustments each time you write an email.

TRACKING CLICKS

Some autoresponders allow you to enable or disable the tracking clicks feature. You should *always* track clicks for your emails, every time. You always want analytics data so that you can see what's working and what's not working and adjust accordingly.

If you're not happy with your autoresponder's analytics, or you just want more analytics data, you can use bit.ly or Google's URL shortener at www.goo.gl to shorten any links in your email and get analytics on how many clicks the link receives.

Note: I recently worked on a major book launch where we used goo.gl shortened links to promote the book. After a few hours of massive traffic, goo.gl mistakenly disabled the link and redirected it to a page that said it might be spam. We lost thousands of visitors that day and a lot of money simply because we used a 3rd-party link instead of a regular link. If you're working on a major launch, be wary of using a shortened link from a 3rd-party service that can deactivate your link at any time. After this very bad experience, I probably won't use shortened links anymore.

CREATING AN AUTORESPONDER EMAIL SERIES

You can use autoresponders to create an evergreen sales system that will automatically connect, educate, entertain and sell your email subscribers on your most important evergreen products and services.

Every time you create a new email list, you should create at least one new autoresponder email that your subscribers will receive as soon as they sign up for your list. I recommend creating at least 4-5 emails in each autoresponder series to make sure you're actively building a relationship with your newest email subscribers.

AUTORESPONDER EXAMPLE

I'm going to share with you an example of an autoresponder series I recently created to help promote one of my newest books *The Book Marketing Bible* and build my list quickly using paid traffic from Facebook ads.

I had several goals with this campaign:

Build my email list faster by offering an awesome free report (an excerpt from *The Book Marketing Bible*).
Get more sales and reviews for *The Book Marketing Bible*.
Build up my subscriber base and listeners for The Publishing Profits Podcast Show (http://publishingprofitspodcast.com/).

Attract more highly motivated, educated and talented clients for my publishing company, TCK Publishing (http://www.tckpublishing.com/).
Sell other educational products in the future.

When you start a new email marketing campaign, take a moment to write down your goals and ideal outcomes. Get clear on what your marketing budget is and what results you expect. The clearer you are upfront about what your goals are and what resources you have, the more likely your campaign will be profitable.

AUTORESPONDER EMAIL #1 CASE STUDY

Hey there,

Welcome to the TCK Publishing community!

You can download your free report on 10 Ways to Sell More Books Online right now here: http://bit.ly/10WaystoSellMoreBooksOnline1

You might also want to check out some of our interviews from The Publishing Profits Podcast Show (http://publishingprofitspodcast.com/).with bestselling authors like Hugh Howey who has sold over 1 Million self published books.

You can check out all the free interviews at www.publishingprofitspodcast.com

You can also subscribe to the show on iTunes at http://bit.ly/PublishingProfitsPodcast

Stay tuned on the email list for more tips on writing, publishing and marketing your books.

If there's anything I can do to help you in the meantime, just respond to this email and I'll be happy to help!

To your success,

Tom Corson-Knowles

#1 Bestselling Author of The Kindle Publishing Bible Series

Founder of TCK Publishing

Autoresponder Email #1 Overview

In the first autoresponder email you send to your subscribers, it's important to do several key things:

1) Welcome subscribers (let them know they're part of a community and something special)
2) Deliver what you promised (your free report or free training videos, etc.)
3) Offer more education (an extra bonus with even more information)
4) Give a preview of things to come (let them know what to expect)
5) Keep it personal (don't let your email look like a boring corporate memo that no one wants to read)

Autoresponder Email #2 Case Study

Hey,

I wanted to make sure you were able to download and read your free report on 10 Ways to Sell More Books Online right now: http://bit.ly/10WaystoSellMoreBooksOnline1

Many of you were asking for more info and training about Marketing Strategy #1 in the report on building your email list.

So I created some free tutorial videos for you to explain more about how autoresponders and email marketing work, and how you can start building your own email list for free right now.

You can watch the tutorial videos on email marketing for free on YouTube at www.youtube.com/playlist?list=PLK_bMOz0qH7yBTru1aZpybv6feqEOiR5D

If there's anything I can do to help you in the meantime, just let me know.

To your success,

Tom Corson-Knowles

#1 Bestselling Author of The Kindle Publishing Bible Series

Founder of TCK Publishing

AUTORESPONDER EMAIL #2 OVERVIEW

In this email, I'm again sending the link to the free report because I really want my subscribers to read it. I know that the report is so valuable for anyone who wants to sell more books that as soon as my subscribers read it, they will be hooked and want more.

I'm also going out of my way to provide even more value for my subscribers with detailed email tutorials on the biggest challenge they were having – how to build an email list.

Then, in the P.S., I'm letting them know they can buy my book *The Book Marketing Bible* for even more information on marketing.

Remember, one of my key goals with this campaign was to increase sales of the book. But instead of just pitching the new book with a "hard sell," I'm providing tons of valuable information, and letting my subscribers know they can buy the book if they want to learn even more about marketing strategies that work right now. They already know I sell books. I'm just providing a link to buy my book for those who want to learn even more about marketing. No over-the-top sales copy needed.

AUTORESPONDER EMAIL #3 EXAMPLE

Hey there,

Today I want to share with you three awesome ways to sell more books *right now* without any additional traffic.

Whether you're a brand new author with only a few sales or an experienced author with thousands of raving fans, these three simple tips will help you sell more books *without any additional traffic, fans, or promotion.*

In fact, all you have to do is make three small tweaks in 5 minutes to start getting more sales from your existing fan base:

1. Link to your squeeze page

The first and most powerful strategy is to link to your squeeze page inside your book. (If you don't know what a squeeze page is, go

watch my free video training videos on email marketing at www.
youtube.com/watch?v=E7ZrrMiJbq4&list=PLK_bMOz0qH7yBTru-
1aZpybv6feqEOiR5D)

You can link to your squeeze page at the very beginning of your
book (usually underneath the copyright information on the title
page), and at the end of your book (usually either before or after
your author bio.)

In my experience, adding a link to your squeeze page will turn
3% to 10% of your readers into email subscribers. That means, if
you sell 1,000 books, you'll have 30 to 100 new email subscribers
using this method - for free!

Imagine how this one simple strategy could transform your
business and your career as an author.

2. Link to your other books

If you have other published books, link to them at the end of your
book. If readers liked one of your books, they'll probably like your
other ones, too.

This is a great way to increase sales, and it won't cost you a dime.

If you only have one book right now, that's okay! Keep writing,
and when you publish more books, make sure to add a link to all of
your published books in each book.

3. Ask for a review

Everyone knows that more reviews can help you sell more books.
But one of the often overlooked sources for reviews are existing
readers *while they are reading your book.*

At the back of your book, simply insert a review request. If you
don't know what to write, just copy mine:

> *"Thanks for reading! If you enjoyed this book or found it useful I'd
> be very grateful if you'd post a short review on Amazon. Your sup-
> port really does make a difference and I read all the reviews person-
> ally so I can get your feedback and make this book even better.*

Thanks again for your support!"

Note: Do NOT bribe readers to leave a review. It is against Amazon's TOS (Terms of Service) to offer anything in return for a review, other than a review copy of your book.

Offering to give someone a free report, discount, deal, or any kind of gift in exchange for a review could get your book removed from Amazon and your account banned for life. Do NOT make that mistake!

All you have to do is simply ask your readers to leave a review.

No bribes necessary.

To your success,

Tom Corson-Knowles

Founder of TCK Publishing

P.S. In my book *The Kindle Publishing Bible,* I share more awesome (and free) ways get more reviews, as well as a powerful book launch strategy that can get you hundreds, thousands, and even tens of thousands of downloads in a week.

Autoresponder Email #3 Overview

This email is pretty long, and I wouldn't recommend sending an email much longer than this because you want your subscribers to read your emails completely, and you don't want to exceed their attention span. If someone is busy or distracted and sees a very long email, they may just delete it to clear their inbox.

In this email, I'm continuing to add value and further educate my subscribers. Instead of doing so by only linking to content as in the previous emails, I'm providing the education directly in the email. I like to mix it up so that my subscribers don't get used to either only reading emails and not clicking links, or only clicking links and not reading the emails.

Notice, I also provide a warning about what NOT to do. I think this is really important. If you're going to be a thought leader in your field and educate people about how to achieve their goals, whatever field you're in, it's important to teach them what to do as well as what not to do. Often, simply avoiding a mistake can save people a lot of money and time. You don't need to know 1,000 different marketing strategies if you go broke before you can implement any of them!

Furthermore, there are people in my industry who are giving misinformation, and telling authors they need to offer something in exchange for a review to get more reviews. This is against Amazon's TOS, and can get authors in a lot of trouble. I want to be the one who gives out accurate, valid information, and I certainly don't want my loyal subscribers to make a big mistake like that.

Obviously, this is a big win for my subscribers. But it's also a big win for me. If someone on my list makes a huge mistake and their account gets banned, they may get upset and quit. If they quit, they won't continue to read my emails and buy my books and other products and services. *When you have your subscribers' best interests in mind, ultimately you'll do what's in your best interest by helping them get what they want and need.*

Don't get greedy or stingy with your information. Share it freely, and educate your subscribers as best you can. If you do that well in your emails, they will naturally buy your other products and services because they will want to learn more from you.

Finally, in the P.S. of email #3, I again link to my book, but this time it's a different book that offers a solution to a different problem.

AUTORESPONDER OVERVIEW

Writing autoresponders isn't rocket science. There are elements of both science and art in crafting a great autoresponder series.

Here are some of the keys every good autoresponder series should have:

1. MASSIVE VALUE

Your emails should be incredibly valuable. Either you should provide great education and information directly in your emails, or link to free videos, articles, or other content in which you educate your subscribers. The businesses that add the most value and serve the most people win in the long-term.

2. Offer Additional Products or Services

In addition to adding massive value, you should make an offer for your subscribers to check out at least one of your additional products or services. You don't have to do this in every single email (and you probably shouldn't), but you do need to do this at least once in every autoresponder series.

So, whether there are 5 or 50 emails in your autoresponder series, at least one of them should link to a product or service you have for sale.

If all you do is add value and don't offer anything for sale, you will train your subscribers not to buy from you. That's not good for business long-term. On the other hand, if all you do is sell and promote your products but don't provide any value, your subscribers won't stick around for long. They key is to find that balance that fits for you and your audience.

3. Be Personal

In your emails, write like a real person writing to a real person. Use personal language like "you" and "I." Avoid impersonal language, and don't write like a robot or a corporation. When I write an email to my list, I imagine I'm writing to my best friend. Keep your emails warm, energetic and authentic. However you think a typical Fortune 500 CEO might write a memo, do the opposite.

The more human and personable you sound in your emails, the more you will connect with your subscribers. The more you connect with them, the more they will like you. And the more they like you, the more they will buy from you. It's also a lot easier, more fun and authentic to just be yourself when you write instead of pretending to be someone else.

How Often Should You Email Your List?

Every email marketer must decide for themselves how often they want to email their list. Some marketers send daily emails, while others send weekly or monthly updates.

Personally, I prefer to send about one email a week on average. Sometimes I send more, and sometimes less. I don't worry too much about it. Friends don't email friends every week at 2pm on Wednesday, so why would I email my subscribers on such a rigid schedule? For some businesses, sending regularly scheduled emails makes perfect sense, especially if your subscribers are expecting certain information at certain times (like daily weather updates or weekly sports scores). For my business as an author, sticking to such a rigid email schedule isn't the best fit. You'll have to decide what schedule is best for your business.

For example, if I'm traveling or on vacation, I'll usually take a break and do not send any emails to my list. Then, when I get home I'll maybe share a quick tip or lesson I learned on my trip, and reconnect with my tribe.

If I'm working on a major launch, I may email my list several times during the week to give them updates and keep the launch excitement going.

Don't Let Your List Get Cold!

Whatever you do, make sure to stay in touch with your subscribers on a regular basis. Ignoring your list and not sending an email for weeks or months can turn your list cold fast. They will forget about you, forget how they signed up for your list, and start ignoring your emails. One of the biggest mistakes you can make with email marketing is not emailing your list regularly and letting it get cold.

I've seen it happen to several people, and it turned a super valuable business asset (their list) into an almost worthless liability.

If you have no idea what to send your subscribers, just email them a survey and ask about what they want, what they need, what problems and challenges they're facing and what kind of solutions they're looking for. This will keep you connected with your audience and give you ideas for new products, services, trainings and other things you can do to help your subscribers.

Updating Your Autoresponder Series

It's good practice to update your autoresponder series every few months. In my business, every six months I go back through all my autoresponder emails and edit, update, tweak, delete, change or rewrite them as needed. You'd be amazed how much can change in just six months.

As you learn new things, create new products and services, and get feedback from your audience, continue to update your autoresponder emails so that they stay fresh, relevant and current. This doesn't mean you have to completely rewrite every single autoresponder email! But definitely check and make sure your emails are not out-of-date, that all your links are still working, and that your autoresponder series is helping you meet your business goals.

If you find your autoresponder series isn't meeting your goals after 3-6 months, it's time to make some changes.

Remailing

With an autoresponder, you have the option to remail to subscribers who don't open an email, or don't click on the links in an email.

This can be a very powerful tool during a major launch or promotion, and here's why:

Let's say you send an email on day 1 of your launch announcing your new offer.

On day 3, you check your autoresponder analytics and notice only 30% of your email list opened the first email. What you can do then is send a remailing to the 70% of your subscribers who did not open the first email. If they didn't open the first email, that means they don't know about the launch.

If another 30% of your list opened the 2nd email, you could then remail a third time to the remaining 40% who didn't open emails #1 and #2.

Remailing allows you to keep promoting a launch to your subscribers who don't know about it without bothering the subscribers who already know about it by sending them multiple emails.

In general, if you're working on a major launch or promotion, I recommend remailing at least once to all your subscribers who didn't open the first email.

In my experience, remailing to subscribers who didn't open the first email usually results in a 15-30% increase in sales during a major launch or promotion. Needless to say, I was thrilled when I first learned about this strategy and implemented it in my business for major promotions.

CHAPTER 8

PRODUCT LAUNCHES, PROMOTIONS AND SWIPE COPY

Whenever you're working on a major product launch or promotion, your email list will be one of your greatest assets to drive sales and get the word out.

In this chapter, you'll find a few tips and ideas I've learned the hard way over the last several years on how to get the most out of your email promotions.

DISCOUNTS

If you ever plan to offer a discount on your product, make sure your email list gets the best deal. Nothing will turn off email subscribers faster than learning that they paid $997 for your product while you were offering someone else's subscribers the same deal for just $497.

If you don't plan to discount your product, then you have nothing to worry about. But, if you do discount your product, always ensure that your email subscribers get the best deal.

EXTRA BONUSES

Providing extra bonuses only for your email subscribers is a great way to increase sales and provide even more awesome value for your audience. While doing a major promotion, you could email your list and write something like this:

> *"Since you're a loyal subscriber, I wanted to make sure to provide a little something extra to say 'thanks!'*

So here's what I'm doing. If you grab my new product right now (include a link to your product), I'll throw in an extra bonus. You'll also get this other really cool product. This bonus is only for email subscribers, and it is NOT listed on the website.

Because this is a super-secret bonus just for subscribers like you, you'll have respond to this email with your receipt after you've purchased the product, and we'll send your bonus right away. "

Adding an extra super-special bonus just for subscribers can be a great way to add more value and build a deeper relationship with your list without offering a price discount. It's a win-win for everyone, and it's a great way to increase rapport with your subscribers.

Affiliate Promotions and Swipe Copy

If you become an affiliate for another company's product or service, you may want to promote their products to your email list. You should only do this when the product is high quality and very valuable to your audience. Sending bad affiliate offers is one of the quickest ways to burn out your email list and damage your relationships with your audience.

The easiest way to ensure that a product is good is to test it out yourself. If you've never heard of the product before or used it, ask the owner to give you access to the product so that you can try it out, and if you like it, then you will recommend it to your audience. Sometimes this special access for affiliates is called "Affiliate Access," or "JV Access" (JV stands for Joint Venture). If you have no experience with the product and the owner will not give you JV Access, you probably should not be promoting that product unless you have a close relationship already and really trust the product owner (but then again, if you had a close relationship, they should give you access to review the product).

Once you've chosen a great product to promote to your list as an affiliate, the product owner may send you swipe copy. Swipe copy is essentially a pre-written email that the owner recommends you send to your list. The swipe copy will usually contain everything you need to send the email including your affiliate link, but there's no industry standards for how to write swipe copy. Because there are no set standards for swipe copy, and because copywriting skills vary greatly, you should never just blindly copy and paste swipe copy and send it to your list.

Instead, you'll want to check several things. The checklist below will help ensure that when you send swipe copy to promote a product, you do it properly without making a mistake.

CHECKLIST FOR SENDING SWIPE COPY

1. Make sure it's a great product.
2. Make sure the email salutation is written properly.
3. Test to ensure your affiliate link is working properly.
4. Rewrite the swipe copy to sound like your voice and ensure that it's the right message you want to send to your audience.
5. Make sure to include your proper signature at the bottom of the email.
6. Test the email by sending it to yourself before sending it to your list.
7. If the test looks good, send it to your list.

CHAPTER 9

BACKING UP YOUR EMAIL LIST AND OTHER LIST MANAGEMENT TIPS

You should regularly back up your email list to ensure that you don't lose your valuable list of subscribers. This gets more and more important the bigger your list gets. Once your list is big enough, it really makes sense to invest some money and/or time in doing everything you can to back up your list at least twice to reduce your risk of losing it in an accident or if your autoresponder provider goes bankrupt or gets hacked, or something else bad happens to it.

We talked about redundancy before when it came to using analytics. Redundancy is important when it comes to analytics, but it's crucial when it comes to safeguarding your email list and most important business assets. If you want your business to thrive and survive through changes, it's important to have redundancies built in so that if something bad happens, you can recover as quickly as possible. Everyone has setbacks in business. It's a natural part of the process. The more prepared you are, the faster you can get back on track and keeping moving forward after setbacks occur. That's why it's so important to regularly back up your email list.

There's a slightly different process for backing up your email list based on which autoresponder you're using. Just email your autoresponder support team or google "how to backup an email list with [insert name of your autoresponder]" and you should find a tutorial on how to do it with your particular autoresponder.

Once you've downloaded the file with your backed up email list(s), make sure to save that file in a cloud-based secure folder such as Dropbox. You should also create a physical backup on a flash drive or backup hard drive just in case. Remember, redundancy is important to protect yourself and your business from potential catastrophic loss.

You should probably back up your email list monthly. Some large online marketers back up their email lists weekly or even daily.

Let's assume an email subscriber is worth $5 to your business. Losing a list of 1,000 subscribers would be a $5,000 loss. If you want to avoid that kind of loss in your business, back up your email list!

The larger your list and the better your relationship is with them, the more valuable it will be and the more often you should back it up to avoid a significant loss.

THE VALUE OF YOUR LIST
The value of an email list varies from person to person and business to business. Generally speaking, your list is more valuable if:

> *It's bigger*
> *You have a better relationship with your subscribers*
> *You have more products and services to offer*
> *You have a better marketing funnel*
> *Your list is more targeted*
> *Your list consists of proven buyers who have either bought products or services from you or a similar business recently*
> *How often you email your list (the more often, the better in many cases)*
> *How many of your subscribers actually open and read your emails*
> *…and more*

Because there are so many factors that affect the value of your list, there's no way I can tell you how much your list is going to be worth to your business.

In my experience, my email list is far more valuable than my Facebook pages, Twitter, Instagram, and Pinterest platforms combined. Whenever I launch a book, product or service, email marketing is usually one of the top, if not the top, source of sales.

Don't let small numbers in the beginning discourage you. Everyone starts out at zero and has to grow from there. I've seen entrepreneurs create six-figure businesses with only one product, 1,000 email subscribers and some hustle.

Cleaning Your List

From time to time, you will probably want to clean your list and get rid of old subscribers who don't receive or open your emails.

Some email marketers say that you should never delete a subscriber just because they don't open your emails. You never know – they just might open up one of your emails some day and buy something from you. Pretty much everyone agrees, though, that any undeliverable emails should be removed from your list.

Some autoresponders will automatically remove these undeliverable emails after a period of time, while others may not.

Personally, I remove all undeliverable emails as well as all emails from subscribers who have been subscribed for more than 6 months and have not opened an email in at least 6 months. One thing you definitely don't want to do is delete your active email subscribers, however. To avoid making a mistake, call your autoresponder customer support team and ask them to walk you through the process of deleting ONLY your unsubscribed or inactive subscribers.

What to Do with Your List of Unsubscribed Emails

When you start building a significant list of email subscribers, you will naturally get people who unsubscribe. That's just part of the game, and it's absolutely normal so don't feel upset or take it personally when you see how many people unsubscribed from your email list. But what should you do with all these unsubscribed emails?

Personally, I never sell, rent, or give out my email subscribers' information to anyone, ever. I delete all unsubscribed emails on a regular basis along with undeliverable emails and subscribers who haven't opened any of my emails in the last 6 months or more.

I would highly recommend NOT selling, renting or giving out email addresses for any of your subscribers. Whatever you decide to do with your email subscriber information, make sure it's clearly stated in your privacy policy. Some marketers would say that deleting these emails is a lost opportunity for profit, but for me the profit from my good reputation is worth far more than what I might gain by selling my subscriber's information.

PRIVACY POLICY

A privacy policy is a statement or a legal document that discloses some or all of the ways a party gathers, uses, discloses and manages a customer or client's data. If you're going to be building an email list, you need a privacy policy.

Typically, privacy policies are written by attorneys who specialize in this field.

Although I can't give legal advice and I'm not an attorney, I know that some email marketers have started out by simply googling "privacy policy template" and using a free online template to create their privacy policy. Your privacy policy should be hosted on your website, and there should be a link from any of your squeeze pages to your privacy policy (it should be the only link on your squeeze pages in most cases.) Make sure you link to your privacy policy on any website you own that hosts your opt-in forms.

In your privacy policy, you need to let your customers and subscribers know what you plan to do with their emails. If you plan to sell, rent or give their emails to 3rd-parties, that must be clearly explained in your privacy policy. Again, I can't give legal advice, so it's best you consult with an experienced attorney who can help you do handle your legal matters the right way.

GOT QUESTIONS?

If you have questions about email marketing, feel free to reach out to me and I'll be happy to help answer them. You can reach me at www.tckpublishing.com/contact

Note: Please don't ask me questions about the technical details of using a particular autoresponder or software package as I probably don't know the answer. The best place to get technical support is from your Autoresponder's or software provider's customer support staff or forums. That said, I'm happy and willing to answer any general questions about email marketing strategy for you.

HELPFUL RESOURCES, TOOLS, SERVICES AND LINKS

Leadpages (https://www.leadpages.net/)
Aweber (http://www.aweber.com/)
Launchrock
Mailchimp (http://mailchimp.com/)
GetResponse (https://www.getresponse.com/)
Infusionsoft (https://www.infusionsoft.com/)
Samcart (https://samcart.com/)

SPECIAL FACEBOOK GROUP

Come join our Facebook group just for readers like you who want to take their marketing to the next level. In this group we'll be sharing our successes, marketing tips and strategies with each other so that we can all continue to grow our businesses together.

This is also a fantastic group for finding joint venture partners and cross-promotion opportunities! Imagine if you had thousands of other entrepreneurs from all over the world collaborating with you–imagine how big of an impact you could have.

It's also a great place to get any marketing questions you have answered as well.

Come join us here on Facebook: www.facebook.com/groups/KindlePublishers

CONNECT WITH TOM

Thank you so much for taking the time to read this book. I'm excited for you to start your path to creating the life of your dreams as a Kindle author.

If you have any questions of any kind, feel free to contact me at www.tckpublishing.com/contact

You can follow me on Twitter: @JuiceTom

And connect with me on Facebook: www.tckpublishing.com/facebook

You can check out my publishing blog for the latest updates here: TCKpublishing.com

I'm wishing you the best of health, happiness and success!

Here's to you!

Tom Corson-Knowles

ABOUT THE AUTHOR

TOM CORSON-KNOWLES is the #1 Amazon best-selling author of *The Kindle Publishing Bible* and *How To Make Money With Twitter*, among others. He lives in Kapaa, Hawaii. Tom loves educating and inspiring other entrepreneurs to succeed and live their dreams.

Get the free Kindle publishing and marketing video training series from Tom here: EbookPublishingSchool.com

OTHER BOOKS BY TOM CORSON-KNOWLES

Destroy Your Distractions

Email Marketing Mastery

The Book Marketing Bible: 39 Proven Ways to Build Your
Author Platform and Promote Your Books on a Budget

Schedule Your Success: How to Master the One Key
Habit That Will Transform Every Area of Your Life

You Can't Cheat Success!: How The Little Things You
Think Aren't Important Are The Most Important of All

Guest Blogging Goldmine

Rules of the Rich: 28 Proven Strategies for
Creating a Healthy, Wealthy and Happy Life and
Escaping the Rat Race Once and for All

Systemize, Automate, Delegate: How to Grow a Business
While Traveling, on Vacation and Taking Time Off

The Kindle Publishing Bible: How To Sell
More Kindle ebooks On Amazon

The Kindle Writing Bible: How To Write a Bestselling
Nonfiction Book From Start To Finish

The Kindle Formatting Bible: How To Format Your
Ebook For Kindle Using Microsoft Word

How To Make Money With Twitter

101 Ways To Start A Business For Less Than $1,000

Facebook For Business Owners: Facebook Marketing
For Fan Page Owners and Small Businesses

How To Reduce Your Debt Overnight: A Simple System
To Eliminate Credit Card And Consumer Debt

The Network Marketing Manual: Work From
Home And Get Rich In Direct Sales

Dr. Corson's Top 5 Nutrition Tips

The Vertical Gardening Guidebook: How To Create
Beautiful Vertical Gardens, Container Gardens and
Aeroponic Vertical Tower Gardens at Home

ONE LAST THING...

Thanks for reading! If you enjoyed this book or found it useful I'd be very grateful if you'd post a short review on Amazon. Your support really does make a difference and I read all the reviews personally so I can get your feedback and make this book even better.

Thanks again for your support!

Printed in Great Britain
by Amazon